THE TEARS THAT WATER MY YEARS

Amber Gibson

BookLeaf Publishing

India | USA | UK

Presentation by *BookLeaf Publishing*

Web: www.bookleafpub.com

E-mail: info@bookleafpub.com

ISBN: 9789358369342I

First edition 2023

DEDICATION

First and foremost, I would like to dedicate this book to the most special person in my heart, my reason for living, my son, William Gibson. Thank you, Will as you have grown into a young man, I could not be more proud of you. May God bless you and keep you safe, no matter near or far, I, your Mother will be watching over you, and praying for an amazing future, you truly deserve it.

Additionally, my Grandma Chastain who has been the cheerleader of my life, since the day I was born, along with my grandparents, who passed in 2007. Last, but not least, my parents, for loving me unconditionally.

ACKNOWLEDGEMENT

I would like to say a special thanks to my birth mother, who gave me the love and talent for writing, though not discovered until well after her passing, she has been an influential part of my thoughts and heart.

Additionally, I am ever so thankful to Mrs. Shelia Phipps for the many years of being there and encouraging me in good and difficult times. She made a promise to her friend (my mother) thirty-three years ago and through love, compassion, brutal honesty, and prayer never once lost sight of that promise.

Lastly, I would like to thank my friends and family, who have encouraged me to put my writing out there over the years. To the ones, who heard me when I was quiet and who prayed for me in private as the years passed by. Thank you!

A Mother's Love

A mother's love is second to none
I did not understand this until I had my only one

A mother's love is gentle and true
Guiding her child in the right thing to do

A mother's love is her best trait by far
Praying in the moment and healing every scar

A mother's love is missed when she leaves this earth
Never replaced, worth all worth

A mother's love is felt all along life's way
Never to fade, never to stray

Onward and Upward: Goodbye to the High School Days

Today you will walk those halls one last time
This morning I woke to write you this rhyme

You may feel sadness as you walk past friends
and say
"I'll miss you, but see you around one day"

The truth is, that you may never again
Today remember to hug and love each one of
them.

You will smile at those who supported you, and
look at others with disgrace
Know that everything that's happened, God
already had set in place.

Those halls, that you hated walking some days,
may make you shed a tear
Not knowing why you feel like that, and how
you will hold those halls so dear

You have conquered and endured more than
anyone thought could be
Persevering in hardship, and have become the
young man, that "coach" couldn't see

This chapter is completed, and the ceremony and
celebration to come
I want you to know, today, if needed, you are
allowed to feel a little numb.

Change is hard and the unknown is a scary
place.
All I'll ever ask of you is to set your own pace

Don't take on the weight of the world, as you
have seen your mother do
Continue to be kind and show up for those, who
have and will show up for you

I pray good things for you, always and forever
Your dedication and work ethic, will forever
now be measured

I'm glad you have it in your heart, all the love
that you do, it will follow you to the next chapter
You can do whatever it is, you choose to do.

Today will be a bag of mixed emotions, that so
many have felt before…

Happiness, sadness, the need to explore
Wishing you the best last day, as you open and
close that door.

Those halls helped shape you, and the people
within
Can never be taken, the memories with dear
friends

SOAR

The day I dropped him at college...

I leave you here with wings to soar
Knowing I'm leaving you with so much more

A heart of gold to do what's right
So many watching over you with all their might

Knowing as I go, blessings you will find
Be patient with yourself, as you give it all some
time

Make the best in the weeks and years to come
Meet new friends and don't drink the rum

Your future starts now, I've given what I've got
I'll be by your side always, carry with you the
lessons I've taught

Be kind to others, think with your heart
Remember money, doesn't always lead to a head
start

Your willingness to learn and your work ethic
are true
All of these traits will see you through

My Son

My son is funny, it's easy to see
Always likes to come in first, or in a bad mood
he may be

He works hard when the subject interests him
If it does not, he will complete it on a whim

He is a special soul to so many others
In my home never had any sisters or brothers

He holds a special place in this mother's heart
Been my number-one fan right from the start

Very worldly, this boy, and knows too much for
his own good
Sometimes this hinders him as we all know it
should

He gets along with most, but for some, he just
can't
You will quickly know who because he tends to
rant

He is so happy 90% of the time.

Everyone soon figures out when they have
crossed his line

Physical aggression is something you will rarely
see
Not to say it doesn't happen but it's few and far
between

He knows how to save and knows how to plan
For most of his life, he has had to act like a man

I see him so happy when he is out on a field
Whether baseball or football he strives to
become more skilled

His heart is heavy at times because of his dad
He hasn't been in his life much and I can tell he
is sad

I try to make up for the lost time with him
He sees his father's time with him becoming
slim

I can't change all that and try not to bother
Just continue down my path of being a Mother
and Father

Will knows it's a struggle just he and I at times

But he knows whatever he needs I'd spend my
last dime

He is not spoiled, and aware money doesn't
come easy
That boy understands life isn't always breezy

He often thanks me for the sacrifices I've made
I can't help but look at him, smile, and assure
him I'm unafraid

For we are both aware that God will see us
through
And for now, that is my son… the best I can do

A Heart to Young

Since ninety-one, I've looked up at the sky
Given a little nod, my way of saying hi

Knowing you watch over me throughout every
day
I've wished for so long that you could have only
stayed

You were my Mother, who left me too soon
I will never forget the first time, I walked back
into my room.

I found it clean, and the church ladies did well
I just knew things were different, like a new type
of hell

I had lost my mother, what did that mean
Still think the little girl I was, forever would try
to be seen

That type of loss, few understand
How jealousy attacks the heart seeing a mother
and daughter hand in hand

As the years go by, I miss her more and more

Wondering what it would have looked like, what she had in store

She would be my best friend, with the loving heart she had
Not a doubt in my mind, her smile would make hard days not so bad

In the woods now, just thinking of her and I
At this very moment, a tear falls from my eye

I looked up just now, high into the trees
Still is my heart as I watch a red cardinal sing

As sad as it's been, as hard as times get
I wouldn't ask her back here, to sadness and regret

A beautiful place her soul rests I know
I'll live life for her here, try to be her glow

My Mother

I knew a woman who did all she could
To help the poor and turn bad into good

She would do anything to help you in any way
In the middle of the night or beginning of the
day

We all loved and needed her, but God needed her
more
He took her and opened the pearly gate door

He gave her wings and a halo so bright
And told her to shine the stars at night

She is unlike any other
Because that angel is my MOTHER
-          Darci 1973

The Mistruth of Time

Give it some time, you will be okay
Thirty-one years later and much to my dismay

Time, it heals no wounds, that's true
You must learn a new way of life, and how to
make it through

It is not easy, at best it's a chore
Waking each day, in and out the door

Hoping to remember, anything from years past
Never knowing when they will appear, or how
long the memory will last

Memories are all I have, to guide me each day
Hanging on tight, trying not to lose my way

People don't know, it's hard for some to fathom
Not realizing so much loss can disrupt your
enthusiasm

Loss of a loved one, carrying the emotional
sword
All I know for sure, is ya have to trust in the
Lord

He will find a way to always carry you through
Be a guiding light toward a land where all will
be made anew

His grace, and His mercy, are the guide to life
Showing you paths that may relieve some strife

Walk Don't Stay

You had me for a moment and chose to let me go
Looking back now, I think you finally know

You come around from time to time, making
sure I'm aware
That you search for me, day and night, looking
anywhere and everywhere

I told you this would happen, I knew that'd be
the case
When you find true love, you can't allow it to go
to waste

I begged and I pleaded with you to make it all
right
I waited and waited, hoping you'd see I was
worth the fight

You walked away from me and now you ask me
why
When songs come up, you tell me that you cry

What can I do now, it's over and done
Why do you say things, thinking still you've
won

I loved you for a moment, you chose to walk away
Don't tell me your heartbreaks now, mine has every day

Stand By Me

At times I'm wrong, and sometimes I'm right
Regardless of my stance, I'll always fight

For my way is my way, and you can't tell me it's
not
I'll forever feel this way, not worrying about
being caught.

Time will tell those who stand by my side
Always there along for the ride

People are strange in all their ways
Just passing along throughout their days

You could be right, but won't always be
Just stay and stand alongside me

Where Does One Find Love

Is it in the darkest of nights with a wanderer by
your side
At the foot of the bed where your mother gave
your life

A crowded street where a stranger sought you
out
In a moment of darkness when you only felt
doubt

Was it the day that your sins were washed away
Maybe on a creek bank that you wish to be on
every day

Was it through a phone, when someone called
you in the morn
At your lowest when you were tattered and torn

Was it a day, you can't remember so well
Do you still feel it, only you can tell

Maybe you have it hard right now, maybe you're
on the right path
Wherever you may be, just realize life always
has wrath

You've had love, it's been there in your face
You may often forget it was God's saving grace

So be here now, let the moment seep in
You've had love all along, it comes from within

Forsaken

In a world of trouble, in a world of pain
Day by day I am not the same

I see you reaching out, and I back to you
Then one day realize your absence is true

This isn't too one, many have been lost
Different reasons, and seasons, all at a cost

Friendship held tightly, I forever will adore
Then the time comes to close another door

Sad in this moment, another place unknown
Why would you forsake me after all the things
you've shown

Feeling Love

It's been asked "Why you can't feel love"
Being let down is my answer, to the question
above

Truth and openness were all I ever asked
I hope he sees this time, that he can't have a pass

My heart is aching my cheeks are filled with
tears
He was aware, I would have given him my years

Tomorrow's a new day and a new life to lead
I'll see what that consists of, but tonight
emotions bleed

Alone on the river knowing no one can call
I knew better when I heard his silence, he was
bound to let me fall

What a sad day when it all comes to an end
What heartbreak and angst when you realize
you've lost a friend

A friend you were there when things got tough
for them

A friend who did you wrong over and again

I should stop writing these feelings, they won't
mean much in the end
Realize that sometimes there's no use in amends

Alone again now and how I plan to stay
God someday will guide me to find another kind
of way

A way to feel loved by someone who doesn't
leave
Tonight, I guess it's my time to grieve

Another disappointment another love lost
That one had me settled above all other costs

He has had more chances than anyone given
I'm alone again, keeping all the facts hidden

I was always honest and never wanted to hide a
thing
Believed in my heart he was doing the same

Decisions

Today she decided she won't want you anymore
To her, you were just another to walk through an
open door

She gave you what she could, as her time would
allow
Never once asking, if, when, or how

She's lost in her thoughts with each passing day
But knows in her heart it's truly the only way

You let this one down and have time and time
again
The only thing she begged, was a forever best
friend

Her heart feels guilty when she tries to move on
Stops it the split second thinking maybe you are
not gone

He hates when she puts things in the third person
as only she knows to do
But that's the way her feelings come out not for
her, but for you

She has tried over and over to make you
understand
The feelings she has for you the ones that you
can mend

How did you let it go so easy, no hurt and no
shame
Why did you make her think it was only her to
blame

She has tried to hold on with no doubt in her
heart
Waiting for a real chance to have a real start

These words she writes are all taken with the
breeze
When she realizes she dated just another sleaze

With that said she's letting it all go
Don't ever come back because her heart will
know

It will remember how you let her down with
words never spoken
How your actions left her bruised and
emotionally broken.

Take your life and be the best you can be
She will cheer you on, I know because she is me

A Walk in the Woods

A walk in the woods would do you some good
Take a break from reality, really you should

Take a look around
All there is to be found

Venture in the morning, and the evening too
See the nature around, the blue skies, the hue

Watch for the birds, relish the trees
Find peace in your heart, follow the breeze

Do not wait for tomorrow do it today
Take a walk in the woods, it will help you find
your way

Runaway Girl

I walked through the door a thousand miles from
home
Running away from everything, needing to
freely roam

I saw you play, that first night on Duval
Hopped onto the stage, hoping not to fall

The next night was Geiger Key fifteen miles out
It may have seemed I stalked you, but it was fate
without a doubt

There you were, strumming once more
Right along that Key West shore

Numbers were shared then laughter and such
Who would have thought we would do so much

Pirate museum, bars, sunset, and a drink
Talking of dreams, families, just things to make
us think

Then one more show, or so I thought
We ended up entangled at your place, no worries
if we were caught

My how those few days quickly flew by
When it came time to go, I walked away with a
sigh

I flew home refreshed, a smile on my face
Wishing I'd had more time to spend with you in
that space

I'm thankful it was you, the man on the stage
Doing what you do, just earning your wage

A Friend in Me

I left you in your chaos, that's where you needed
to be
Let you sober up, to figure out, what you like
about me

I didn't use you, like so many would do
Got you home safe, and expected nothing from
you

I see your heart, dear man, I understand your
pain
You've not spoken of it much, though I believe
we are the same.

I'm never going to be that girl that just hops into
your bed
I can only let you know how much I truly care
instead

Take this as you will, put some thought into it
for a bit
Whatever it is you do, promise you will not quit

Two end loaves of bread is not at all what you
are
I'm sorry you feel like that when you're more of
a shining star

I wish we could sit down, and talk real for a few
I just know when I look into your eyes, I see part
of me in you.
It's hard to explain, though I know I could
I just want you to know your worth, as so many
others should

You know if you need a friend, I'm only a phone
call away
Just remember yourself, find happiness, and
leave others to their own dismay.

The Porch

Washing and cleaning, keeping them strong
I will vow to do this all day long

You have left a hole, that no one can replace
With all the chaos around, I needed to see your
face

You didn't come around any corner, the porch
you did not enter
I just waited around for you, like so many
winters.

I can't believe you're gone now, you and your
heart of gold
If you could only have known all the
possessions I'd have sold

Just to have you here today, the porch there was
a plenty
Honoring your life, your heart, you know there
were many.

People laughing and smiling all around
I look into the distance, again nowhere to be
found.

I'll miss you tomorrow the same as today
If there's peace in your heart, what more is there
to say

Rest easy my guy, for now, you are free
I'll treasure our friendship, all the things you
instilled in me

The Reminder

Those hands that once held you, are still so near
He asked I take care of you, though made it very
clear

He is watching over you, his only sweet girl
You must remember, that he is still in your heart,
in your world

Mistakes we do make and we forever will
Always stand tall, but take some time to stand
still

Do not make excuses, do not be ashamed
Do not place fault, never place blame

We are who we are, and who God intended for
us to be
Happiness and love my dear are what he wants
you to see

Life is so precious, and hands always fade away
Thankful for the years they guided you, along
life's hard highway

Cling to this moment, cry out deep within your
heart
Remember that a father's love can never tear
apart

You hold that head up, you have nothing to
explain
I'm always here to listen, stand by you, and ease
your pain

I believe in you, and all that you are
Take a step back my friend, another day isn't far

The Unknown Cure

She loads the dishes, takes the trash to the curb
Never once excepting for him to say a word

She mows the lawn when he has too much to do
Pays his tuition as her Father asked her to

She is his mother and sometimes he doesn't
understand
How hard it is for her to find for him a loving
man

She is a failure in herself, to her there is no
reason
She just sits back and waits, she says for the
perfect season

Someday she will see how, how she let him
down
She looks at him and sees there is not a lot on
his crown

Knowing in her heart of hearts he didn't deserve
the pain
A life without a father, who else is there to
blame

She always fought for him, her son, and in his
heart was pure
Could it be that she has failed him, never to find
a cure

A Chance to Say

If I could have you back, for only a minute or
two
I'd hug you ever so tight until you turned blue

I'd make you laugh for a second, and ask how
you've been
Shed a tear or more and think about way back
when

If I could have you back, for only a minute or
two
We could sit outside, looking around at all the
new

I would accept the fact that you couldn't stay
long
You've got a grander place to be, where there is
no wrong

If I could have you back, for only a minute or
two
I would have a chance to say goodbye
something I never got to do

A Moment Today: Memorial Day

To our men and women who lost their lives in
war
You gave us all you had, your life, it is no more

In the world's harshest times, you helped set the
future free
Gave your life defending this land, for your
family, and also for me

Memorial Day, sad, just another day for some
My heart always thinks back, at times
completely numb

Thinking of your eyes and the last thing they did
see
How scared must have been, begging God
"Please save me"

Sending all the gratitude, your soldier heart
never heard
I do this in my head never speaking an actual
word

Praising your sacrifice, deep within my soul

If only you were here to hug, only then would
you know

You've not been forgotten, a promise for sure
The world is as fragile as ever, and people still
looking for the cure

Free we still are, due to your lives indeed
Enjoying what you had to sacrifice, dying hearts
left to bleed

www.ingramcontent.com/pod-product-compliance
Lightning Source LLC
LaVergne TN
LVHW012155060726
842759LV00028B/846